THE ROLES OF GOVERNMENT AND INDUSTRY
IN RESEARCH AND DEVELOPMENT FOR THE
MARITIME INDUSTRIES

An Interim Report of the
Committee on Strategies to Improve R&D
and Its Implementation in the Maritime Industries

Marine Board
Commission on Engineering and Technical Systems
National Research Council

National Academy Press
Washington, D.C.
1986

NOTICE: The project that is the subject of this report was approved by the Governing Board of the National Research Council, whose members are drawn from the councils of the National Academy of Sciences, the National Academy of Engineering, and the Institute of Medicine. The members of the committee responsible for the report were chosen for their special competences and with regard for appropriate balance.

This report has been reviewed by a group other than the authors according to procedures approved by a Report Review Committee consisting of members of the National Academy of Sciences, the National Academy of Engineering, and the Institute of Medicine.

The National Research Council was established by the National Academy of Sciences in 1916 to associate the broad community of science and technology with the Academy's purposes of furthering knowledge and of advising the federal government. The Council operates in accordance with general policies determined by the Academy under the authority of its congressional charter of 1863, which establishes the Academy as a private, nonprofit, self-governing membership corporation. The Council has become the principal operating agency of both the National Academy of Sciences and the National Academy of Engineering in the conduct of their services to the government, the public, and the scientific and engineering communities. It is administered jointly by both Academies and the Institute of Medicine. The National Academy of Engineering and the Institute of Medicine were established in 1964 and 1970, respectively, under the charter of the National Academy of Sciences.

This report represents work supported by Cooperative Agreement No. N00014-82-C-0032 between the Department of the Interior and the National Academy of Sciences.

Limited copies are available from:

Marine Board
Commission on Engineering and Technical Systems
National Research Council
2101 Constitution Avenue
Washington, D.C. 20418

Printed in the United States of America

COMMITTEE ON STRATEGIES TO IMPROVE R&D AND ITS IMPLEMENTATION IN THE MARITIME INDUSTRIES

George F. Mechlin, Jr., <u>Chairman</u> (NAE)
Westinghouse Electric Corp.
Pittsburgh, Pennsylvania

Daniel Brand
Charles River Associates, Inc.
Boston, Massachusetts

William A. Creelman*
Marine Consultant
St. Louis, Missouri

Jose Femenia
SUNY Maritime College
Bronx, New York

Ernst Frankel
Massachusetts Institute of Technology
Cambridge, Massachusetts

Andrew E. Gibson
American Automar, Inc.
Washington, D.C.

William J. Harris (NAE)
Texas A&M University
College Station, Texas

John H. Leeper
Phillips Cartner & Co.
Alexandria, Virginia

Frank W. Nolan, Jr.
ITO (retired)
Essex Fells, New Jersey

Edwin J. Petersen
Todd Pacific Shipyards Corp.
San Pedro, California

Milton Pikarsky (NAE)
City College of New York
New York, New York

Robert N. Steiner
Port Authority of NY/NJ
New York, New York

Robert J. Taylor**
Exxon International (retired)
Satellite Beach, Florida

John F. Wing
Booz, Allen & Hamilton, Inc.
Bethesda, Maryland

H. Peter Young
American President Lines, Ltd.
Oakland, California

Staff

Charles A. Bookman
Assistant Director for Programs

*Resigned from the Committee, August, 1985.
**Resigned from the Committee, February, 1986.

MARINE BOARD
of the
COMMISSION ON ENGINEERING AND TECHNICAL SYSTEMS
NATIONAL RESEARCH COUNCIL

Bramlette McClelland, <u>Chairman</u> (NAE)
McClelland Engineers, Inc.
Houston, Texas

William C. Webster, <u>Vice Chairman</u>
University of California
Berkeley, California

Roger D. Anderson
Cox's Wholesale Seafood, Inc.
Tampa, Florida

Robert D. Ballard
Woods Hole Oceanographic Institution
Woods Hole, Massachusetts

William M. Benkert
U.S. Coast Guard (retired)
McLean, Virginia

Kenneth A. Blenkarn
Amoco Production Company
Tulsa, Oklahoma

Donald F. Boesch
Louisiana Universities Marine
 Consortium
Chauvin, Louisiana

H. Ray Brannon, Jr. (NAE)
Exxon Production Research
Houston, Texas

Robert G. Dean (NAE)
University of Florida
Gainesville, Florida

Charles D. Hollister
Woods Hole Oceanographic Institution
Woods Hole, Massachusetts

Peter Jaquith
Saint John Shipbuilding, Ltd.
New Brunswick, Canada

Kenneth S. Kamlet
URS Dalton
Washington, D.C.

Don E. Kash
University of Oklahoma
Norman, Oklahoma

William M. Nicholson
U.S. Navy (retired)
Annapolis, Maryland

Ernest L. Perry
Port of Los Angeles (retired)
Sun City, Arizona

Richard J. Seymour
University of California
La Jolla, California

William H. Silcox
Chevron Corporation (retired)
San Francisco, California

Richard T. Soper
Sea-Land Service, Inc.
Iselin, New Jersey

Robert J. Taylor*
Exxon International (retired)
Satellite Beach, Florida

<u>STAFF</u>

Ralph D. Cooper, Director
Charles A. Bookman, Asst. Director
Donald W. Perkins, Asst. Director
Richard W. Rumke, Senior Staff Officer

Martin J. Finerty, Jr., Staff Officer
Doris C. Holmes, Admin. Associate
Joyce B. Somerville, Admin. Secretary
Aurore Bleck, Senior Secretary

*Resigned from the Marine Board, February, 1986.

FOREWORD

This year marks the fiftieth anniversary of the passage of the Merchant Marine Act of 1936. The act fosters development and encourages the maintenance of the U.S. merchant marine by providing that the United States shall have a merchant marine:

(a) sufficient to carry its domestic water-borne commerce and a substantial portion of the water-borne export and import foreign commerce of the United States and to provide shipping service essential for maintaining the flow of such domestic and foreign water-borne commerce at all times, (b) capable of serving as a naval and military auxiliary in time of war or national emergency, (c) owned and operated under the United States flag by citizens of the United States insofar as may be practicable, (d) composed of the best-equipped, safest, and most suitable types of vessels, constructed in the United States and manned with a trained and efficient citizen personnel, and (e) supplemented by efficient facilities for ship-building and ship repair.

This national maritime policy has been implemented through direct and indirect subsidies, promotional programs, research and development (R&D), and in other ways. While the specific elements of government maritime programs have been altered over the years to address conditions of the times, the underlying policy remains essentially unchanged.

Fifty years after this act was passed, the U.S. maritime industries are undergoing unprecedented change as the result of an eroding U.S. competitive position in world shipping and trade, deregulation of the transportation industries, and increasingly fierce competition for discretionary government funds. In the face of these changed (and changing) circumstances, it is appropriate to assess the programs that implement national maritime policy.

This report, prepared at the request of the Maritime Administration (MarAd), addresses the question of the importance of fostering the development and application of technology in the maritime industries (i.e., shipbuilding, ship operating, marine terminal operations, and inland waterway operations), and the roles of industry and government in this. It is an interim report of a larger assessment of the health and status of R&D in support of enhanced productivity and international competitiveness in U.S. maritime industries.

This report addresses the R&D process in the maritime industries in a very broad sense with the intent of including all aspects of the creation and commercial application of technology, ideas, and concepts that contribute to equipment or operations relevant to the maritime industries.

The assessment is being conducted by a committee appointed by the National Research Council and operating under the auspices of the Marine Board. Members of the committee were selected with regard for the expertise necessary for the assessment, and to achieve a balance of experience and viewpoints on transportation technology development and application in general, and in the maritime industries in particular. Committee members' backgrounds span the fields of R&D management, users of technology (ship operation, shipbuilding, ports, terminals, and inland waterways), technology development (industry and academia), technology transfer, government maritime policy, and R&D in other industries. Biographies of the committee members appear in Appendix A. The principle guiding the constitution of the committee and its work, consistent with the policy of the National Research Council, was not to exclude the bias that might accompany expertise vital to the study, but to seek balance and fair treatment.

This interim report concludes the first phase of the committee's activities in which working groups of the committee prepared background papers on the state of technology development and application in each of the economic sectors being addressed. Members of the working groups made a substantial contribution to the committee's deliberation; they are listed in Appendix B. The background papers reviewed industry status and identified needs. The development and application of technologies relevant to the needs, and the roles of industry and government in addressing these needs were then assessed. The reports of the working groups support and substantiate the interim report.*

---

*Single copies of the working papers are available from the Marine Board, National Research Council, 2101 Constitution Avenue, Washington, D.C. 20418.

An overall objective of the committee, extending beyond this interim report, is to identify, appraise, and recommend alternative approaches to improving the health and status of R&D in the maritime industries. From an evaluation of the business climate of the maritime industries, an examination of the existing R&D programs in and for the industries, and an estimate of the effects of public sector policy and private sector business strategy, the committee will synthesize a set of predictions as to who the future sponsors of maritime industrial R&D might be (or might not be) and what the expected business and national benefits of such R&D might be (or might not be). The committee will also consider the role of current or new financial incentives, existing or new organizations, and also more aggressive government, industry, or collaborative sponsorship and facilitation of maritime technology development and application. An important judgmental input to this is an evaluation of the national consensus concerning the future need for a U.S. maritime industry. Beyond its purely naval aspects, this consensus appears to be both vague and wandering. The committee's final report will be publicly available early in 1987.

George F. Mechlin
Chairman

CONTENTS

1. SUMMARY AND CONCLUSIONS 1

   Private Sector Roles 4
   Public Sector Roles 4
   Discussion of the MarAd R&D Program 5
   Recommended Changes in Direction 6

2. THE ROLES OF INDUSTRY AND GOVERNMENT IN THE R&D PROCESS ... 7

3. U.S. MARITIME INDUSTRIES: STATUS, TRENDS, AND NEEDS 10

   Status 10
   Trends 11
   Needs and Opportunities 12
      Shipbuilding 12
      Ship Operating 12
      Marine Terminals 13
      Inland Waterways 14
   Other Considerations 14

4. TECHNOLOGY DEVELOPMENT AND APPLICATION IN THE
   MARITIME INDUSTRIES 15

   U.S. Shipbuilding Industry 15
   U.S. Ship Operating Industry 18
      Containerization 19
      Effective Manning 20
      Ship Management and Handling 21
   U.S. Marine Terminal Industry 22
      Channel Depth 23
      Labor-Management Relations 24
      Equipment and Facilities 25
      Computer Systems 26
      Bulk Terminals 27
   U.S. Inland Waterways Industry 27

5. CONCLUDING OBSERVATIONS ON INDUSTRY AND GOVERNMENT
   MARITIME R&D 31

APPENDIX A: BIOGRAPHIES OF COMMITTEE MEMBERS 35

APPENDIX B: WORK GROUPS OF THE COMMITTEE 41

APPENDIX C: LEXICON 43

SUMMARY AND CONCLUSIONS

Research and development (R&D) are widely recognized as essential instruments in the nation's efforts to maintain its competitiveness in the world economy. The R&D process in the maritime industries (i.e., shipbuilding, ship operating, marine terminal operations, and inland waterway operations) encompasses a broad array of developments and commercial applications in hardware, operating methods, and information and management systems. This report addresses the importance of fostering the R&D process in U.S. maritime industries, and the roles of industry and government in this.

The starting point for an assessment of the importance of R&D in the maritime industries is an understanding of present conditions in the maritime industries in the United States and the world. A global maritime depression has affected all sectors of the maritime industries for 5 years, and shows few signs of a turnaround. Despite this, development and application of new technologies in the U.S. maritime industries have continued to a considerable extent, primarily as a result of intense competition. Several collaborative R&D programs, which have been sponsored in partnership with industry by the MarAd, also have spurred innovation. A list of the most significant technology developments and applications of the last decade would include: advances in shipbuilding industrial processes, improved utilization of the seagoing work force leading to more effective manning and crew reduction, introduction of fuel-efficient diesel engines into U.S. commercial vessels, utilization of state-of-the-art technology in cargo handling and the operation of marine terminals, and a trend toward truly intermodal freight transportation networks in part a consequence of government deregulation. There is also, for the first time in a decade, at least a glimmer of hope for renewed public investment in capital improvements to the nation's harbors and waterways. These developments, the driving forces behind them, their principal benefits, and the roles of industry and government in the past and in the future are summarized in Table 1.*

---

*Not all of these developments and applications have been won easily. In nearly every instance formidable barriers in the area of government regulations, business conditions, management attitude, labor and management relations, and environmental constraints have had to be overcome.

TABLE 1 Overview of R&D in the Maritime Industries and the Roles of Industry and Government

Industry Sector	Current Driving Forces	Key Technology Developments	Principal Benefits	Principal Developers and Their Roles	Future Needs	Future Roles
Shipbuilding						
Commercial	Reduced government support; Lack of cost and financing competitiveness; Loss of government support	--	--	MarAd sponsored collaborative program with industry facilitated technology transfer	Improve price competitiveness; More economic-lot-size production	Government and industry need to address national policy issues of industry support and competitiveness
Navy	Fleet expansion; Cost control	Improvements in shipbuilding process technology	Savings in hundreds of millions of dollars in the construction of naval vessels in the last 5 years	Shipyards developed and applied technology; Navy provided contract incentives to improve; MarAd sponsored collaborative program with industry facilitated technology transfer	Further computer applications and advances in process technology; Reduce overcapacity; Promote management-labor cooperation	Navy continue contract incentives; Navy collaborate with industry on advances in process technology and computer applications; MarAd continue collaborative program with industry
Ship operating						
Liner	U.S.--largest trading nation creates market; Deregulation of freight transport opened competition	Containerization; Effective manning; Fuel efficient engines; Management systems; Jumbo ships; Inland feeder systems	Favorable impact on operating expenses	Containerization has been led by U.S. entrepreneurs; Manning, engines, and management systems development have been led by foreign companies. MarAd has facilitated technology transfer and labor-management cooperation	Further operating, cost, and service improvements; Modernize pertinent regulations to make them supportive of fleet modernization; Control labor costs	Industry will pursue incremental improvements as a result of competition; MarAd should document need and be catalyst for rationalizing regulations
Bulk	Overcapacity; Aging, expensive U.S. fleet	Fuel efficient engines; Management systems	Favorable impact on operating expenses	See above	See above	See above

TABLE 1 (Continued)

Industry Sector	Current Driving Forces	Key Technology Developments	Principal Benefits	Principal Developers and Their Roles	Future Needs	Future Roles
Marine terminal	Labor-management conflicts; High cost of terminal labor; Increased competition; Trend toward intermodal transportation; Deregulation of freight transportation; Local-federal, public-private cost-sharing	Terminal automation; Incremental improvements in intermodal terminals and technologies; Waterway improvements	Most competitive port wins greatest share of trade in deregulated operating environment	Terminal operators and equipment manufacturers have been responsible for incremental improvements; MarAd-sponsored collaborative program with industry is emphasizing automation testing and technology transfer; Corps of Engineers has been national agent for waterway improvement	Further automation of terminals; Further intermodalism; Further automation of paperwork; Management-labor cooperation, more effective use of human element; Improve national waterway deepening situation by pushing national planning and priority setting, improving national decision making/permitting process, and relying more on cost-sharing; Multipurpose terminals; Utilization of dredge spoil as a resource	Industry will pursue technology improvements as a result of competition. MarAd can facilitate technology application by addressing management-labor improvements, similar to role in effective manning. Customs needs to collaborate with industry on paperwork automation. MarAd can possibly facilitate this. Waterways improvements continue to be primary responsibility of Corps of Engineers, although cost-sharing increases local interest in cost-effective improvements
Inland waterways	Depressed demand; Overcapacity	Waterway infrastructure; Vessel and fleet productivity, as a result of improvements in technologies and management systems	Still cost competitive, although competition from rail and pipeline is gaining	Infrastructure is the responsibility of the Corps of Engineers; Vessel operating companies have been responsible for technology and management system improvements	Reduce overcapacity; Modernize infrastructure; Improve industry-wide data on trade and operations to enable strategic planning	Infrastructure remains responsibility of Corps of Engineers; MarAd-led industry collaboration on data and planning needs may be appropriate because benefits of R&D for any one operator are overshadowed by risks of investment

Table 1 and the material in the report support the following conclusions about the appropriate roles of industry and government in the R&D process.

PRIVATE SECTOR ROLES

Concerning the role of the private sector in maritime research and development, the committee arrived at two conclusions:

1. Industry sponsorship of proprietary R&D is governed principally by the expectation of individual corporate financial gain or a requirement to comply with a regulation in the most cost-effective manner. Individual company sponsorship of R&D has focused to a great extent on activities that have short-term payoffs. In the difficult financial environment that exists today, there is little likelihood that this pattern will change.
2. There is scant evidence of collaborative R&D among companies, except where it has been stimulated by third-party, usually U.S. government agency, activities. Given the financial condition of the industry and its structural fragmentation, there seems little possibility of significant collaborative R&D in the future, unless the government continues to stimulate collaborative R&D.

Notwithstanding the above, companies may be interested in collaborative R&D when the benefits of the R&D process are likely to be applicable to a group of companies and/or the costs/risks of such work are greater than individual firms are willing to bear. More fundamental research not directed to specific product development and technology developments directed at areas of operational interchange among or between companies are particularly appropriate candidates for collaboration.

PUBLIC SECTOR ROLES

Concerning public sector roles, the committee made two conclusions:

1. Government sponsorship of R&D is necessary to support national needs for security, public safety, ports and waterways planning and development, ensuring that the base of scientific and technical knowledge exists to support existing laws, and promoting international competitiveness. In support of these needs, the government:

- Acquires data, conducts feasibility and other analyses, and supports demonstration projects.
- Conducts R&D in support of policy or program development, such as the assessment of technology and implications of current or proposed laws, rules, or standards.
- Conducts R&D that directly benefits the government, such as efficiencies in the handling of government impelled and preference

cargoes or advances in naval shipbuilding technology, which reduce the cost (to the government and the nation) of naval ship acquisition.

2. Government sponsorship of industrial R&D is desirable where it acts as a catalyst to achieve broad national benefit to industry and the nation. Government collaboration with industry is especially appropriate where the benefits of R&D are likely to be applicable across an industry (and will benefit the nation as a whole), and where, whether because of unacceptable risk or for other reasons, proprietary incentives to conduct the R&D are lacking.

DISCUSSION OF THE MARAD R&D PROGRAM

The R&D program of the Maritime Administration (MarAd) has contributed in several ways to improving or maintaining the competitiveness of the U.S. maritime industries. Through collaborative approaches with industry, MarAd has promoted technology transfer in shipbuilding process technology, vessel manning, cargo handling, and fleet operations. It has facilitated the diffusion of innovations and their application, especially where supporting changes in labor-management relations or government rules have been necessary.

The collaborative programs conducted by the MarAd have been appropriate because they have, at relatively small cost, addressed two weaknesses in the U.S. maritime industries. Maritime interests in the United States have been very fragmented between such entities as U.S.-flag and non-U.S.-flag, liner and bulk, operators and builders, and builders and designers. This fragmentation can be traced to competing objectives arising from different operating and regulatory environments, and a history of aggressive antitrust enforcement. In part due to the fragmentation of the industries, the U.S. maritime industries have never developed strong cooperative institutions such as independent R&D centers. Such institutions are common in the maritime industries of other countries.* The MarAd R&D program has sought to fill the role of a technology center for the industry and also has sought to identify and address common R&D objectives in this fragmented industry. Without government participation, the industry-based collaborative R&D institutions that are now in place (as a direct result of the activities of the MarAd R&D Program) are not likely to continue.

Top-level industrial interest in the R&D program of the Maritime Administration has not been extensive, but has been increasing in recent years. Even with this increasing top-level interest and support, it appears that government involvement in maritime R&D will shortly be cut back, perhaps even beyond that which is necessary to

---

*National Research Council. 1983. Ship Operation Research and Development: A Program for Industry. National Academy Press: Washington, D.C.

support the government's functional needs. This would certainly have some negative impact on R&D in the maritime industries. Without government sponsorship, the collaborative programs in shipbuilding, fleet management, manning, and cargo handling are likely not to be continued separately by industry.

To a great extent, the collaborative programs that the government has implemented address derived needs—the identification and prioritization of problems and the development of approaches to them are derived from industry. The success of this kind of arrangement depends on communication. It is necessary, therefore, to develop a process for communication. Periodic top-level review of needs and programs is important. MarAd's collaborative programs have established processes for communication in the development and implementation of technical work programs. Its programs need more emphasis on sustaining top-level communication on industry needs to ensure their continuing relevance.

RECOMMENDED CHANGES IN DIRECTION

In summary, the R&D program of MarAd should direct:

● Greater effort in support of the government's functional needs. A particularly promising area is providing the technical basis for modernizing laws, rules, or standards that adversely affect the capacity, productivity and cost-effectiveness of the maritime industries.

● Greater effort to identifying industry needs with top-level industry management. Through collaboration with industry, MarAd should continue to sponsor R&D where government sponsorship acts as a catalyst to achieve broad national benefit to the maritime industries and the nation.

Regardless of the direction of future activities, it is essential to maintain at least a minimum level of funding and program activity, if the U.S. government is to maintain its technical capability to understand and reap the benefits of technology developments in the world maritime industries. Furthermore, it is essential to continue to monitor technological developments around the world and to make that information available to U.S. industry.

For their part, the highest levels of U.S maritime industrial management should demonstrate their interest in and support for the R&D process on a continuing basis, with MarAd, in industry forums, as well as within their own companies. Without top-down direction and involvement, continued investment and leadership in maritime R&D by government and industry cannot reasonably be expected.

THE ROLES OF INDUSTRY AND GOVERNMENT IN THE R&D PROCESS*

In the United States, there appears to be a general consensus that the private sector is the preferred sponsor of business activity. As a corollary, it is concluded that the government should refrain from direct participation, or sponsorship of economic enterprise, other than in exceptional circumstances. However, in certain areas, the exceptional circumstances appear to be sufficiently prevalent as to dim, if not to obscure, the principle. Certainly, in the maritime industries, the complexities of government versus private sector roles are especially pronounced. The U.S. maritime industry as it exists today (similar to maritime industries of other countries) only partially resembles a market driven economic entity either in its relationship to the U.S. government or to its international competition.

In general, industrial sponsorship of research and development is governed principally by the expectation of financial gain. There is an observable coupling between business conditions and the funding of these efforts with the short-term financial needs of the business frequently receiving priority over the long-term expectations of the research and development.

Historical experience demonstrates that the government's role in sponsoring R&D is important in three areas:

1. Where the government requires technology to execute its statutory or constitutional responsibilities. Defense is, of course, an obvious and well-understood example.

2. Where the general public benefit or impact on the public in terms of safety and environmental quality is great and no other sponsorship could be expected. The sponsorship of basic research in universities through the National Science Foundation and the National Institutes of Health is an example. The accomplishments in this area

---

*The term "R&D Process" refers to the creation and beneficial application of technology. A lexicon of related terms appears in Appendix C.

are very significant and indeed can be said to be the envy of the world.

3. Where the beneficiaries are numerous, but small and otherwise incapable of systematic research and development sponsorship. Agriculture is the classic example of this class of research and development.

From time-to-time, the government has chosen to define a role for itself in other areas. Energy R&D has been a recent example that was based on the perception of an immediate, significant, and socioeconomically damaging energy shortage. The program included major efforts at both technology creation and application. When the shortage failed to materialize, the government revised its policy. Today, only the higher risk portions of the technology creation still are being supported, and these at steadily decreasing levels. Similar decreases in government support for the R&D process are taking place in many industries, including the maritime industries.

Under certain circumstances, collaboration in the R&D process is desirable. Collaboration among industrial companies is appropriate when the benefits of the R&D process are spread across an industry or the costs or risks are higher than individual companies can bear. Government and industry collaboration is appropriate and desirable where there are compatible goals in the broad national interest. This is particularly true where international competitive or national security issues are directly involved. Most observers agree that the U.S. aerospace industry owes it international preeminence to massive U.S. government-sponsored R&D and procurement. Table 2 summarizes the respective roles of industry and government in the R&D process by establishing a spectrum of types of proprietary and collaborative arrangements.

In the past one hundred years, the U.S. merchant marine, in total or in part, has been requisitioned to carry out U.S. foreign policy in four major armed conflicts and numerous smaller actions. Furthermore, the competitive performance of U.S. industries, including the maritime industries, in global competition is an important factor in the overall health of the U.S. economy and hence affects our national security. For these reasons it is appropriate for the MarAd, the agency charged with encouraging the maintenance of the U.S. maritime industries, to encourage the development and application of most cost-effective technology by industry and the conduct of most productive operations. An important means of accomplishing this has been and continues to be sponsorship of R&D in partnership with industry.

TABLE 2. Types of Research and Development and Their Characteristics

Characteristics	Industry Proprietary	Industry Collaboration	Industry/ Government Collaboration	Government Sponsored	Government Proprietary
Availability of Results	Sponsoring company	Industry participants	All publicly available	All publicly available	Government
Purpose	Service, product, or cost advantage	Management information or cost savings	Various support	Government policy or function support	Government policy or function
Funding	Sponsoring company	Industry participants shared	Government/ industry cost	Government	Government

U.S. MARITIME INDUSTRIES: STATUS, TRENDS, AND NEEDS

STATUS

The U.S. maritime industries (i.e., shipbuilding, ship operating, marine terminals, and coastal and inland waterways shipping and shipbuilding) are in the midst of rapid change as the result of an eroding U.S. competitive position in world shipping and trade, deregulation of the freight transportation industries, and increasing competition for scarce government funds. One consequence of these changes is the oversupply and overcapacity of capital assets, including ships and barges, shipbuilding capacity, and in some cases underutilized marine terminals. Some of the oversupply/overcapacity is nominal--too many or too much. In other instances the oversupply/overcapacity is structural--the surplus facilities are too old or poorly sited for modern conditions. The problem of oversupply/overcapacity adversely affects the business climate in the maritime industries.

The business climate for U.S.-flag shipping is both depressed and intensely competitive, with excess capacity high on the list of causes. Any time any segment shows signs of profitability, as did the U.S. cruise business several years ago, foreign shipbuilders and the governments that support them produce additional tonnage for virtually any owner. The result once again is oversupply. Given the long list of failures that such a shipbuilding policy has generated, many of the developed countries are reassessing the wisdom of continued support of shipbuilders, with the result that closings are taking place at an accelerated rate.

The mounting losses incurred by the shipowners has hit the international lending institutions particularly hard. Recent difficulties of several major shipowners have sent shock waves through the banking industry. It will be increasingly difficult for even the soundest shipping companies to obtain financing in the future. This will lead to further diversification out of the industry.

As a defensive move, many European ship operators are "flagging out" existing tonnage or selling off their fleets and chartering in cheaper third-flag vessels. This indicates that time has run out on their efforts at cost reduction for their national flag ships. Given the existing overtonnaging, freight rates have plummeted to a point where any tax or regulatory burden or crew cost differential cannot be absorbed. Many owners have concluded that neither the available systems nor the technologies exist that can produce sufficient increases in productivity in the short run to offset the cost differential enjoyed by the third-flag carriers.

A new generation of 4,000 twenty-foot equivalent unit (TEU) container ships is now servicing the United States. This additional low-unit-cost transportation capacity virtually guarantees that 1986 will be another year of depressed freight rates. The demise of well-established shipping companies is likely to continue.

Although the dollar has begun to weaken against the major currencies, the lag time built into foreign trade transactions precludes any substantial change in U.S. trading patterns in the short-to-mid term. For example, there is no recognized forecast indicating any major improvement in the U.S. grain and coal export picture that is essential for a substantial increase in traffic on the rivers. Existing overcapacity also will continue to depress freight rates in this area as will the reduction in the world price of petroleum. The drop in oil prices has also dampened activity in the oil service and supply sectors, and the shipbuilders and repairers that serve that industry. No improvement is in sight.

TRENDS

The U.S. maritime industries are faced with a continuation of trends already well begun. The most competitive shipbuilding and ship operating companies will certainly survive. The surviving ship operators, in particular, will become part of a highly competitive international industry, but much of their expansionary efforts will be in the intermodal land transportation systems so that the ship itself will continue to be deemphasized.

The domestic fleet will continue to shrink and some changes may take place in the cabotage laws, particularly as they pertain to the requirement that all vessels be U.S. built. Because of increasingly competitive land transport alternatives, the higher cost of some Jones Act services can no longer be passed along to the consumer. At present, the cheaper tug-barge systems are taking over, but some provision for foreign building is inevitable in the future.

Many state governments appear to be willing to continue to stimulate port improvement and expansion through the use of state-backed industrial bonds, tax incentives, and subsidies. This will sustain a competitive environment that puts pressure on port costs and at the same time will result in excess port capacity nationwide.

There is a growing concentration of cargoes at a smaller number of ports. This concentration is caused by the necessity of improving the utilization of capital-intensive ships, double-stack trains, and modern marine terminals. To increase the number of vessel voyages and unit train round-trips, carriers must limit the number of port and terminal stops. Load centers have developed around high capacity, high service-frequency ports that offer throughput efficiencies. The growing number of container double-stacked unit-trains has benefited the U.S. carriers that introduced them by substantially reducing inland costs.

The concentration of ship operating activities is hardly good news for some shipbuilders. The largest shipbuilders are sustained with Navy work; the smaller shipbuilders must develop new markets or go out of business.

NEEDS AND OPPORTUNITIES

Even in this depressed climate, there are a number of opportunities for improvement that could add to the overall profitability of segments of the U.S. maritime industries.

Shipbuilding

Given the lack of any significant commercial market, the principal beneficiary of increased efficiency or improved shipbuilding and ship repair techniques is the U.S. Navy. A number of worthwhile projects are being undertaken to accomplish this. These projects constitute a collaborative effort within the industry, with government sponsorship. Despite such efforts in process technology (where benefits accrue to the government in the form of reduced costs for building and overhauling naval vessels), U.S. shipbuilders have just begun to scratch the surface of opportunities that could be created through market research, development of new products, and entry into new markets. An example of this is the industrial plant and floating plant market, which is already creating employment for some U.S. shipyards. Private collaborative opportunities to exploit the foreign market for these units are available through the use of export trading companies and foreign trade zones.

Without government support it will be difficult for the U.S. shipbuilders to be internationally competitive within the foreseeable future. U.S. government assistance in international marketing and in low interest financing of foreign sales is appropriate and necessary. The absence of any international demand for American-built ships, together with high U.S. labor costs, greatly restricts the available market and guarantees an insurmountable price differential.

Ship Operating

Improved utilization of the seagoing work force leading to more effective manning and possibly crew reduction offers a real opportunity for future savings and is being undertaken with the cooperation of some of the U.S. labor unions and the U.S. Coast Guard. A number of the European maritime nations and Japan are well ahead in this effort. Several major U.S. shipping companies are transferring the effective manning technology of Europeans and others into their operations. A MarAd-sponsored R&D program with industry and labor has facilitated advances in this area. The technical basis still needs to be developed for revising maritime education and training curricula and for making manning and licensing changes in the context of U.S. maritime safety regulations.

Long-term efforts relating to energy efficiency are being successfully undertaken by European diesel engine manufacturers and their Asian licensees. Given the limited U.S. market, there is little incentive to undertake independent research in this country; however, U.S. ship operators (and shipbuilders) are monitoring overseas developments and should consider participating in future developments.

Marine Terminals

No significant technological limitations impede marine terminal operations. Most modern container terminal operators are aware of and use the latest technologies when their use is cost-effective. The two most promising areas for productivity improvement in the next five years are advances in automation of information flow within marine terminals, and improvements directed to the performance of the human element, including management and labor.

As in other sectors of the maritime industries, technology development and application in marine terminals is healthiest in certain Asian and European countries. Any shortcomings in performance in U.S. terminal operations compared to foreign operations of similar capability is due more to the performance of the human element—management, dockside labor, organization, and work practices—than it is to a need for new technological development.

Generally speaking, labor has not impeded the technical development and application of most competitive technology in U.S. marine terminals. However, in East and Gulf Coast ports, long standing labor/management agreements have denied much of the cost-saving benefits of new technologies to the terminal operator; this has impeded full utilization. Manning levels of longshore gangs in these areas are two to three times the size of those in most areas of the world, and crane productivity in U.S. terminals is less than that of the most productive terminals in the world. In spite of this disadvantage, terminal operators have continued to innovate, albeit with a resultant squeeze on profitability.

In contrast to other economic sectors of the maritime industries, there is healthy competition in the marine terminals industry between ports, between terminals, and between labor unions. As a result of relocation of ports and creation of new marine terminals, the traditional labor union alignments are being challenged by newcomers to the longshore industry. High labor costs are creating an opportunity for new approaches and organizations and its growth is bound to continue.

Inland Waterways

Since all basic waterway improvements are government sponsored, the lack of funds and time-consuming procedures for approval of waterway projects are major barriers to improvements in operating conditions and business opportunities. Nevertheless, incremental operational improvements that modestly reduce cost and increase service can reasonably be expected, based on past performance. Opportunities for improving the productivity of vessel operations are to be found in advances in the engine room, hull design and materials, improved maneuvering, personnel safety and health, training of personnel, better communications, and eliminating burdensome regulations.

OTHER CONSIDERATIONS

Given the depressed earnings in the maritime industries, any real interest in technology development and application on the part of the industry will only be to identify short-term opportunities for cost saving or market segment enhancement. Additionally, with continued government emphasis on the eventual elimination of all direct subsidies for the maritime industry and reduced federal investment in ports, only projects that further these short-term goals can be expected to have federal support unless they can be presented as essential to national security.

4

TECHNOLOGY DEVELOPMENT AND APPLICATION IN THE MARITIME INDUSTRIES

This chapter presents an overview of technology development and application in the maritime industries in recent years and identifies the roles of industry and government in these endeavors. It addresses the forces that are driving developments, the key developments, the organizational infrastructure that produced the developments, and additional needs of the industry.

The sources of information for this overview were background papers on the state of technology development and application in each of the four economic sectors being addressed--(1) shipbuilding, (2) ship operating, (3) marine terminal operations, and (4) inland waterway operations.

The papers were developed by experts from each of the industry sectors (see Appendix B). The definition of technology development and application in those papers and in this interim report is broad, as has been explained. It encompasses development and commercial application of changes in hardware, operating methods, information systems, and management systems. This broad definition was adopted because it encompasses the types of engineering and operating advances that appear to be important in the maritime industries.

The framework for this chapter is to examine, for each of the four industry sectors, the economic issues and driving forces in the sector, then to identify key technology accomplishments and their benefits, the infrastructure for accomplishment (i.e., how and by whom the work was conducted and implemented), and finally to assess remaining needs and opportunities.

U.S. SHIPBUILDING INDUSTRY

A paucity of merchant shipbuilding and ship repair work is hastening a contraction of the U.S. shipbuilding industry. Even expanded Navy ship acquisition programs require less than the industry's capacity. Shipyard employment, with several exceptions, is down, and several yards have closed.

Intense competition for a limited market has resulted. On a global scale, an increasing number of shipbuilders are chasing a decreasing volume of commercial shipbuilding work. In many instances, foreign governments are making available varied forms of direct and indirect subsidies, as well as liberal credit terms, which enable their shipbuilders to offer favorable prices. The United States is not of the same disposition.

U.S. shipbuilders have not, in modern times, competed in the world market for many reasons. These reasons include disparities of costs of labor, lower productivity, unfavorable foreign exchange rates, stricter laws affecting employment and ship design, separation of design and production segments of the industry, and a lack of support by the U.S. government to the extent that other governments support their shipbuilding industries. Furthermore, the federal government has not provided direct subsidies for commercial ship construction since 1981.

The scarcity of merchant ship work has made shipbuilding, conversion, and repair for the U.S. Navy increasingly important to American shipyards. To this end, a 600-ship Navy that includes 15 carrier battle groups, nuclear submarines, and greater amphibious assault capabilities will be reached by 1990. Most of the ship construction contracts to achieve that objective have been placed. The majority of this work is being undertaken in a handful of shipyards. Four shipbuilders employ approximately 70 percent of the total new construction work force.

The industry has made significant advances in shipbuilding productivity through technology advancements and better management in the design, planning, and production processes, in part as a result of the competitive award of naval shipbuilding contracts with incentives to minimize cost. The MarAd R&D program facilitated the introduction and application of technology advances in U.S. shipyards.

A Navy survey found that many defense contractors will modernize their facilities when contractual incentives and long-term market stability provide a viable base for business investment. Absent these conditions, naval shipbuilders will seek direct government funding for plant modernization.

Since 1983, as a consequence of improved shipyard productivity and lower-than-estimated inflation, some shipyards have been able to deliver ships ahead of schedule and under budget. The costs of some naval ship construction programs have dropped by as much as 34 percent. These savings have been achieved through combinations of facilities improvements, changes in labor/management attitudes, production management systems, advances in construction techniques, and wider use of computer systems in design and production. The shipbuilders themselves have identified and created these opportunities for improved productivity; the necessary investments have come from the shipbuilders with contractual incentives from the Navy.

During 1981, the Navy funded six top-down self-assessment surveys with leading shipbuilders to identify what technologies would improve naval shipbuilding productivity. Shipbuilders submitted technology proposals directed toward improved manufacturing techniques, processes, or machinery. The outcome of the survey revealed that the shipbuilders were extremely conservative in their approach to technology development because barely 6 percent of the 160 technology proposals required production technologies whose feasibility had been proven only under laboratory conditions. The remaining 94 percent of technology proposals mainly called for technology transfer from other shipyards or industries, which could be implemented with minimum risk and delay.

While conservatism with respect to introducing new production technologies in a shipyard environment was evident, considerable production gains have been achieved by the shipbuilders. Some have acted independently, responding to the incentives created by the naval ship acquisition programs; some have obtained direct government funding of advances under the Manufacturing Technology Program of the U.S. Department of Defense; all have benefited from the collaborative National Shipbuilding Research Program.

The National Shipbuilding Research Program is a cooperative venture between the shipbuilding industry and MarAd. It provides financing and management of research projects to improve the productivity of U.S. shipyards and their competitiveness in the world shipbuilding market. The program, initiated in 1971, is financed by both industry and government and provides for industry involvement in technical management and execution through involvement of the Society of Naval Architects and Marine Engineers' Ship Production Committee (SPC). The SPC collaborates with MarAd in the management of the program, especially to set program priorities, assign responsibilities for projects, provide technical direction, and assist in demonstrating program results. Panels of the SPC work to exchange technical information, identify new problems and recommend opportunities for R&D, oversee ongoing projects, and demonstrate completed work. The costs of research projects are shared by the lead shipyard and the government, often on a fifty-fifty basis.

Two developments in shipbuilding technology have great potential and should be advanced by the Navy, shipbuilders, and suppliers. They are integration of engineering and production to support zone-oriented, modular ship construction and the use of computers in shipbuilding.

Shipbuilders, suppliers, and the Navy are introducing computers in the three fundamental areas of their operations: design, manufacture, and production management. Yet, shipbuilders' systems are, in general, considerably behind the state of the art. Because the Navy is the major shipbuilding customer in the United States, it has the obligation to initiate industry-wide innovations that will lead to significant communication and productivity improvements, leaving selection and implementation of computer systems to the shipbuilders and suppliers themselves.

The traditional, adversary relationship between management and labor hinders technology development and application in the shipbuilding industry. Personnel are the most important resource in the ship development and production process, yet until quite recently management and organized labor have shown little interest in working together as an integrated team. Important issues to be resolved in order to maximize efficiency of the shipbuilding process include:

work rule flexibility, cross-craft training and assignment, automation of the shipbuilding process, and employee involvement. The National Shipbuilding Research Program has recently initiated a Human Resources Innovation Program to address these important issues.

In summary, technology developments in the shipbuilding industry focus on manufacturing and production improvements aimed at productivity gains and reduced costs. Considerable progress has been made in the last 5 years in reducing the labor hours in shipbuilding. Navy shipbuilding programs have been the primary drivers for these advances, which have been accomplished by the shipyards. The collaborative industry-government National Shipbuilding Research Program, administered by the MarAd, has served as a principal driving force to plan, organize, and manage this R&D. The program has facilitated technology transfer in this arena, and has funded supporting research and development.

In view of its current role as the most direct beneficiary of improvements to the shipbuilding process, the U.S. Navy would benefit from having within its organization a central focus for collaborating with the shipbuilding industry and with the MarAd on developing and implementing process technology. A shipbuilding technology division was recently established at DTNSRDC, which could fill this role.

U.S. SHIP OPERATING INDUSTRY

As the largest international trading nation, the U.S. presents an immense market for U.S. and foreign ship operating companies. Most U.S.-flag operators have not been cost competitive, but this has not prevented vigorous participation by U.S. operators in the liner trades. This participation was made possible in the 1950s, 1960s, and 1970s by the government's subsidy programs but increasingly in recent years by application of U.S.-developed container technology and intermodal systems.

The U.S. shipping industry includes general cargo and bulk cargo segments. The general cargo sector includes several aggressive containership operators competing successfully for international cargo.

The major East/West liner trade routes are served by modern, large to ultra-large container ships supported by foreign-flag feeder ships and an expanding U.S. and worldwide intermodal network operating under increasingly sophisticated control systems.

The general cargo trade protected by the Jones Act is served mostly by older container ships operating in coastwise trade and to Puerto Rico, Hawaii, and Alaska. The trade also supports a few highly competitive, modern coastwise integrated tug barge systems also operating to both Alaska and Puerto Rico.

The U.S.-flag bulk carrier segment comprises mainly older vessels carrying petroleum, grain, and dry bulk cargoes in the cabotage and Jones Act restricted trades. Few U.S.-flag vessels are operating competitively in the international bulk trades. Most of the vessels operating in foreign trade are subsisting on government-aid cargoes. They are generally old by world standards and require freight rates more than double the world scale, even after subsidy, because of high labor and other costs.

Technology developments in the ship operating industry will be discussed in three areas: (1) containerization, (2) effective manning, and (3) management and control.

Containerization

The transition to containers in liner shipping has transformed ship and port design and operations as well as the economics of ocean shipping. Rapid growth in containerization and intermodalism in the 1970s and 1980s was made possible by several key technology innovations. These included changes in ship configuration, cargo handling equipment, terminals, and rail cars as well as new marketing, operating, and management systems.

The most modern containerships can carry in excess of 4,000 20-foot containers. They are powered by fuel-efficient, slow-speed diesel engines, and have hull forms that minimize resistance and reduce construction costs. Increasing use of automation and restructuring of shipboard work is allowing crew sizes to be reduced.

Both rail and ocean carriers have caused the development and implementation of innovations such as:

- Lightweight, articulated rail cars designed to carry double-stacked containers.
- Automated information systems for processing and shipping data between carriers, shippers, terminals, and third parties.

At ports and terminals, developments have been directed toward more rapid and efficient transfer of larger unit loads between ocean carriers and land carriers.

The container revolution and the evolving intermodal transportation systems are the result not only of technology development; as, or more, important have been the creativity and willingness of managers to take major capital investment risks to gain a competitive advantage. Thus, developments were driven by commercial incentives to increase productivity of physical assets and human resources and to be able to offer better service than competitors.

There has been only modest industry-wide or cooperative research and development in this arena, nor has there been an infrastructure to lead such work. This is hardly surprising considering the highly competitive nature of the U.S. industry and the minimal history of cooperative research in the maritime industry. However, some collaboration motivated by necessity has occurred; examples include the standardization of container sizes and lift points. More recently, MarAd has sponsored a Cargo-Handling Cooperative Program (CHCP) modeled after the National Shipbuilding Research Program. Under the CHCP, U.S. liner operators, which also operate marine terminals, are investigating technologies needed by all, such as systems for automatic identification of containers. Significant advances are being achieved through this cooperative industry-government program.

Effective Manning

At the present time, manning levels for new large oceangoing container ships and single-product tankers are generally in the 18- to 22-person range. Ten to fifteen years ago the manning levels for comparable vessels were in the 30 to 35 range. In some instances, the reductions have been achieved without significant planning; in other cases, there has been considerable joint experimentation and negotiation by management, labor, ship, and shore personnel.

Manning changes require innovations in operating practices and hardware--engine, deck, bridge, food service, and other equipment--as well as fleet management practices. In reducing manning, it is also necessary to address human factors elements, such as the effects of isolation on worker performance and safety. Most of the effective manning advances to date were developed and applied first by foreign ship operators, often as the result of collaborative national programs.

In addition to the technology development required for more effective manning, organizational changes are required based on work redesign. Work redesign refers to deliberate efforts to modify the organization of shipboard work. This might include structural changes such as new billets, new management practices, and revised union work rules. Research to identify the educational and training needs of present-day and future seafarers is needed.

One important work organization change has been that of intradepartmental flexibility in which individuals take on more responsibilities within their own departments, e.g., steward/cook, cook/baker, and electrician/reefer/junior engineer.

Crew continuity, a potentially important manning innovation, is very difficult to achieve in the U.S. merchant marine because of the current surplus of labor. Unions attempt to spread diminishing job opportunities among their members.

Hardware innovations enabling further manning reductions have largely proceeded from foreign shipyards, frequently in association with nationally funded R&D efforts. Shipyards and governments wishing to continue the export of merchant ships are quite aware of customer interest in smallest-crew vessels. As the level of manning drops into the mid-teens, a need develops for significant further technology innovation in hull and machinery maintenance.

In the U.S. ship operating industry, the advances in effective manning are being achieved primarily within individual steamship companies working with their unions. Engineering design organizations have provided guidance on the availability of supporting hardware. Also, MarAd has performed an important catalyst role through sponsoring technology transfer, and facilitating joint labor-management approaches to problem solving.

Ship Management and Handling

A number of ship management functions have been partially or fully automated through use of computers and satellite communication systems with a resulting positive effect on ship management methods and organization.

Ship routing systems were introduced based on satellite weather information, accurate position measures, and onboard and shore-based computer systems that could determine the optimum course and speed for a ship to minimize its fuel consumption while achieving its desired arrival time within acceptable levels of probability. Ship routing systems used various weather and ship progress forecasting techniques. The U.S. Navy has been the principal sponsor of this technology development.

Other important technological developments have been in the area of ship condition management. This refers to implementation of an optimum strategy for fuel and water consumption as a result of monitoring the tanks, stores, and positions of cargo; and computing ship stability, trim, draft, list, bending moment, and shear in near-real time.

Further reductions in manning and auto-pilots controlled by a computer routing/collision avoidance system are expected applications. Other technological changes will probably include remote cargo and ship condition management whereby preprogrammed cargo loading/discharge and ship condition changes are performed without shipboard crew involvement.

Research and development in ship management systems has been performed by commercial equipment suppliers and research firms. MarAd has been a principal sponsor of research in this area through its Fleet Management Technology Program, which has funded research, testing, and implementation work on weather routing, collision avoidance, and other management systems. Many technological advances are fallouts from developments in other areas such as space research, satellite systems, communications research, and automated data base systems.

Interest developed in the early 1970s in the interaction between safety in ship operations and ship handling. This was the result of a number of collisions, rammings, and groundings involving tankers and also vessels striking bridges.

The primary sponsors of research on the safety of ship handling were the U.S. Coast Guard and MarAd with guidance from the Society of Naval Architects and Marine Engineers (SNAME). There has been a continuing R&D effort directed at prediction and improvement in ship handling and controllability. This effort is at a very low funding level after a peak in the mid-1970s. For commercial transportation application MarAd was the major source of funds although these now are minimal. In selected cases, the U.S. Coast Guard and U.S. Army Corps of Engineers have also funded work. The Navy has also supported some basic work in ship controllability which can be applied to commercial vessels. Industrial funding has been very limited.

Ship/waterway interface technology concerns the prediction of ship performance in a particular harbor, channel, or waterway, and the determination of the effects of changes in the waterway on safety or operating efficiency. The driving force behind R&D in this area is harbor/waterway development and maintenance projects. Small changes in channel and turning basin dimensions can have very major cost and environmental impacts. The primary sponsors of research have been MarAd, the Corps of Engineers, and the Coast Guard. SNAME Panel H-10 has continued to provide guidance.

The major tool in this research is the real time, man in the loop, ship handling simulator, of which MarAd's Computer-aided Operations Research Facility is the most advanced in the U.S. Implementation of research in this area has been quite rapid. It has become a standard procedure to use simulators to evaluate alternatives in port and waterway design. Decisions affecting the expenditure of hundreds of millions of dollars for port and waterway construction have been made on the basis of simulator studies.

The shipbuilding and operating side of the industry with few exceptions has made little investment in ship handling research. The most notable exception has been oil company sponsorship of research associated with tanker maneuvering in shallow water in the late 1970s. Fleet management is another area of opportunity. However, the barriers to more effective technology development for the ship operating industry include lack of economic incentives and a weak R&D infrastructure.

In summary, technology developments in the ship operating industry focus on implementation of containerization and intermodal systems, effective manning, and ship management and handling. Containerization, which revolutionized the liner segment of the industry, was developed primarily by operators investing in capital intensive ships and cargo handling equipment spurred by market and profit potential. The next revolution may be in effective manning, with operators and labor trying to catch up with a competitive advantage already achieved by foreign operators. MarAd has played an important supporting role in effective manning technology transfer and facilitation, and in ship management computer systems development.

U.S. MARINE TERMINAL INDUSTRY

Every coastal metropolitan region of the United States centers on a commercial port. The hubs of ports are marine terminals, which are complex networks of receiving, storing, and transporting facilities for cargo carried by ships. At marine terminals, cargo is transferred between deep sea vessels, feeder vessels, and inland transportation modes.

Deregulation on both the land and ocean side has changed the competitive balance substantially. Each element in the transport chain—ocean carriers, inland carriers, and seaport marine terminals—must now stand alone in the shipper's evaluation of least system cost. Furthermore, under the rapidly growing intermodal systems that are developing in the deregulated operating environment, a single carrier may be responsible for the entire routing from origin to destination. Consequently, where past port routing decisions were made on the basis of tradition and legal precedent (under outdated shipping laws), current routings are made on the basis of cost and service performance.

In summary, only marine terminals in those ports that recognize the need to improve productivity will survive the competition heightened by deregulation. Advances in seaport marine terminal technology as well as channel depth, labor-management relations, equipment and facilities, management techniques and computer systems can improve terminal productivity. These areas are discussed next for general cargo terminals as well as bulk cargo terminals.

Channel Depth

The 40- to 45-foot deep channels at the major ports are adequate for virtually all of the largest ships in service or being constructed for the transport of general cargo. The extensive need for landside container storage space, however, has led to relocation of container terminals away from traditional "downtown" shipping centers to outlying areas of ports, necessitating either development of new access channels or deepening of relatively shallow secondary channels. The advantages inherent in the use of large vessels will probably impose pressures for further improvement of the main channels at major ports including the widening of channels for wide-beamed ships.

Channel improvements under today's regulatory environment require resolution of technical problems associated with dredging. Better methods for dredging and removal of dredged materials with minimal adverse environmental impacts need to be developed. The technical basis needs to be developed to increase the utilization of dredged materials and to view them as a resource, as opposed to their current status as a waste material that needs to be disposed of. At estuarial ports, where significant salinity intrusion may result from deepening of a channel, methods have to be developed to prevent contamination of water supply systems that have intakes in the estuary. A means for protecting timber piles exposed by dredging to attack by marine borers must also be devised. Solutions to such technical problems are being sought by the dredging industry and port development organizations.

A major physical constraint to increasing the depth and width of many ships is the limitation of navigation locks in the Panama Canal, the St. Lawrence Seaway, and on inland rivers. The construction of a sea-level canal across the Isthmus of Panama or, alternatively, new locks for accommodating large bulk carriers will, even if adopted, require over a decade to complete.

Alternatives to waterway deepening include the offshore construction of terminals either of man-made platforms or islands in deep water. Another alternative is to serve exceptionally deep-draft vessels at a limited number of ports, each within a major region of the nation.

The use of wide-beamed ships and draft-assistance devices also would avoid the need for channel deepening. Both of these concepts could, however, still necessitate some dredging work.

The principal federal organizations concerned with marine transport and channel works are MarAd, the Coast Guard, the U.S. Army Corps of Engineers, and the Environmental Protection Agency. Several of these organizations sponsor R&D in advancing marine transport and port development. MarAd issues planning criteria for U.S. port development and funds studies on port siting, operating, and financing. It also aids the planning of port facilities and shipping operations by compiling statistics of the nation's waterborne commerce, and updating inventories of port facilities and vessel fleets. One of MarAd's thrusts in technology is its computer-aided operations research facility (CAORF). Located at the U.S. Merchant Marine Academy at King's Point, New York, CAORF simulates navigation operations for the planning of waterways.

The U.S. Army Corps of Engineers conducts a major part of the research on the technical and environmental issues involved in channels, bank protection, and flood control works. The Corps' Waterways Experiment Station at Vicksburg, Mississippi including its Coastal Engineering Research Center is among the few laboratories engaged in the study of hydraulic and sediment regimes, and other phenomena affecting channel development and shore protection. The Corps also conducts research on improvement of dredging equipment and operations.

The EPA and other government agencies have compiled a significant body of knowledge on ways to mitigate the adverse impacts of port and channel projects on the environment. State and municipal agencies, port authorities, and consulting engineers conduct studies oriented primarily to solving technical problems for specific port projects. University researchers also make valuable contributions to understanding the physical phenomena affecting coastal, port, and offshore works.

The main barriers to waterway improvements are a lack of funds and the complicated and time-consuming procedures for approval of waterway projects.

Labor-Management Relations

The application of technology to the operations of the marine terminal industry has had and continues to have a profound impact on the use of longshore labor as well as on labor-management relations within the industry. The use of containers for packaging ship cargo, for example, has prompted significant productivity gains by reducing labor costs and more efficiently using capital assets such as oceangoing liner vessels. To a lesser extent, the introduction of bulk self-unloading vessels, the mechanization of special product carriers such as banana-carrying ships, and the development of other labor-saving technology have all improved the labor productivity of the marine terminal industry. The application of computer technology to terminal management and information processing is also affecting the use and productivity of the work force.

It is apparent that a major labor management challenge facing the marine terminal industry on the Atlantic and Gulf coasts arises from the lack of flexibility in the traditional work rules. The high costs of redundant workers in marine terminals makes this particularly inefficient. It is possible that increased application of technology in marine terminals on the Atlantic and Gulf coasts will be accompanied by the use of a nontraditional waterfront work force.

Equipment and Facilities

Land within ports is in increasing demand. More efficient use of this scarce commodity will be an important area for development in the future.

In the area of marine container equipment and facilities, the major technological developments implemented since 1975 have been improvements in the efficiency of containerized transportation systems. With a few exceptions, notably intermodal operations and technology, there have been no major breakthroughs similar to those seen in the previous two decades.

Some of the technological advancements in the area of containers include designs which are lighter, allow for safer and more trouble-free/maintenance-free operation, and prevent cargo damage. Most of these designs were developed in response to operating feedback of 10 to 15 years of operations with containers prior to 1975.

A particularly beneficial development are containers designed to fit cargo and intermodal transportation requirements more efficiently. High cube containers, 45-foot containers, 24-ton/20-foot containers, and other designs provide economy of scale in the handling of specific cargo for certain trade routes.

Many container terminals do not operate at anywhere near optimum capacity. This is because ports often have caused the development of new terminal facilities for other than economically rational reasons, such as the desire to promote civic image. The only rationalization of terminal usage occurs indirectly through the choice by ship operating companies of the public terminals that they will call at.

The infrastructure supporting technological developments in marine terminal facilities and equipment is varied. Successful projects typically include a combination of government and private sector involvement. Projects completed most quickly and with the greatest impact, however, are sponsored and developed by a single company.

A formidable barrier to innovation in marine terminal equipment and facilities is high R&D costs. These costs are typically too large for one company, port authority, or manufacturer to bear on its own. Millions of dollars of theoretical research, prototype work, evaluation, and analysis may be required to develop an automated piece of handling equipment, for example. Similarly, computer systems development includes major operational impact analyses, hardware and software development, and careful implementation prior to use. Although the system may be cost-effective on paper over a period of time, the resource allocation may be too large for an individual terminal operator or carrier to reasonably undertake on his own. The sophistication and complexity of some projects also often surpass the technological capabilities of any one group. Without sufficient return on investment, engineering developments that originate in the United States are likely to be applied initially overseas.

Attempts to pool resources to surmount these problems have not been successful in the past. There are inherent difficulties in coordinating common or associated entities, such as port authorities, carriers, and manufacturers. Varying profit motives, proprietary notions, and difficulties in focusing a number of individuals on a common goal are typical stumbling blocks.

Another barrier to innovation is the assumed resistance of labor to such change. Some organizations do not implement labor-saving improvements for this reason. In addition, many third-world nations have lobbied in international forums against change, particularly in the area of container development. They fear that once they enter into the fray of intermodal container operations with standard equipment and fixed port facilities, development of more efficient containers and automated ports will make their investments obsolete.

The cost of buying, maintaining, and controlling ocean containers has resulted in renewed interest in break-bulk cargo handling. Highly automated systems for handling break-bulk cargoes have been developed in Europe and will be introduced into the U.S. in the near future.

Computer Systems

Great strides have been made over the last 20 years by using the computer as a management tool. Recently, for example, terminal operators have developed the capability to simulate alternative engineering operations to discern optimum operating configurations. On another front computer systems are being developed to facilitate the movement of freight documentation between brokers, customs officials, and the port authority.

Management systems technology is available to accomplish major gains in terminal productivity, but the major elements--information networking on a grand scale and an electronic identification system for cargo containers--are outside the control of the terminal operator. Standardization and transmission of documents constitute a major area of marine terminal operations awaiting consensus and development.

The majority of companies involved in the operation of marine terminals do not perform R&D. Marine terminal operations frequently rely on external sources for ideas as well as input.

A limited amount of cooperative development and testing is undertaken under the Cargo Handling Cooperative Program established by MarAd in partnership with liner companies.

Bulk Terminals

Technical developments in bulk marine terminals have emphasized increases in speed, capacity, and automation. Considerable improvements have been made in speed and capacity of ship-based, self-unloading cargo handling systems; less dramatic advances have been seen in shore-based systems. Aided by advances in computer technology, bulk handling is increasingly automated. With the aid of programmable controllers, an operator not only can run an entire bulk handling plant but also diagnose malfunctions of any component and prescribe remedies without leaving his control room.

The current profit squeeze in the marine terminals industry has limited application of new technology developments in the United States. Occasionally, new concepts and improvements of existing systems have been developed by engineering companies. The Technical University of Hanover in Germany as well as various manufacturing companies in Japan and Europe have been the main source of recent R&D achievements.

A prime motivation for innovation during the past 5 years has been the growing need for improvement in efficiency and profit in the face of high interest rates and capital shortages. Historically, cargo handling equipment manufacturers undertook a large share of this responsibility, but with severely depressed margins these corporations have not been able to contribute as they had in the past. Much of the recent development work, consequently, has resulted from partnerships between users (such as steel and power companies and operators of facilities) and engineers.

In summary, technology developments in the marine terminal industry focus on channel improvements, labor-management relations, equipment and facilities productivity improvements, and computer systems. Terminal developments have paralleled the container revolution in the liner industry. In the bulk industry, advances in speed and capacity of cargo handling have outstripped the ability of inland cargo systems to accommodate them. Only in the area of channel improvements is there a substantial, established R&D program because, historically, harbor development has been the responsibility of a federal agency--the Corps of Engineers, which has sponsored its own research for its own needs.

U.S. INLAND WATERWAYS INDUSTRY

The Mississippi River and its navigable tributaries are the heart of the commercial inland waterways system of the United States. Intracoastal waterways extend along the Gulf and Atlantic coasts. In the West, the Columbia-Snake Waterway provides shallow draft navigation above Portland, Oregon to Lewiston, Idaho. The Great Lakes and the Tenn-Tom waterway round out the U.S. inland waterways. Nearly 35,000 vessels, primarily barges and towing vessels, operate in the domestic coastal and inland water transportation system of the United States.

The barge and towing industry carry more than 12 percent of the nation's total freight at 2 percent of the total freight bill. The major commodities carried, petroleum and petroleum products, coal, grains, and sand and gravel, can accept the slow delivery of barge movement because of the low cost.

Historically, the U.S. government did not charge water carriers for the use of navigation facilities provided by the government. These facilities include locks, dams, and other improvements on the rivers, locks on the Great Lakes, and harbor improvements on the Great Lakes and on the coast. This policy has been changed. P.L. 95-502 established a fuel tax on inland river carriers beginning at 4 cents a gallon in 1980 and increasing incrementally to 10 cents a gallon in 1985.

Domestic water transportation was a growth industry for the quarter century preceding the decade of the 1970s. During that decade many national and global changes occurred to turn this industry into a mature one due to the construction of excess equipment in certain trades and due to a decrease in the demand for bulk commodities in other trades.

The euphoria of the 1970s has turned into the depression of the 1980s. It is estimated that excess equipment amounts to about 30 percent over what is required and freight rates have plummeted to the levels of the early and mid-1970s. Other problems involve the infrastructure. Locks and dams on the rivers and the St. Lawrence Seaway are in need of replacement and repair.

The industry has until recent years steadily improved its productivity. An important development in towboat design was the adoption of the Kort nozzle, which increases towing ability by directing the flow of water around the propeller. Most importantly, towboats operating on the Mississippi River have increased dramatically in size and power, and tow-handling capability has been improved by the installation of flanking rudders.

Barges have also undergone a similar evolution resulting from early experiments. Steel barges, with streamlined rakes, lessened resistance so that horsepower requirements are from 45 to 60 percent below those of their more cumbersome predecessors. Barge types have been improved; weather-proof covered barges now protect cargoes and tank barges carry all manner of liquids. The barges are designed for minimum resistance in fleet operation.

Breakthroughs in technology or inventions that would revolutionize the operation of river vessels are not expected in the near term. Most of the future advancements will probably be developed by other industries rather than through original development by the maritime industry.

What can be realistically achieved lies in the area of incremental improvements, innovations, and refinements to what already exists. The major areas for opportunities for improving the operation of the vessel are the engine room, hull design, and materials; improved maneuvering; personnel safety and health; training of personnel; and communications.

Hull design and materials improvements result in small increases in speed and fuel savings. Variable pitch propellers and increased use of bowboats and bow thrusters enhance fuel efficiency. More emphasis on training of personnel adds to efficiency and safety.

Telemetry systems, which improve communications between the vessel and the home office, enable the office and vessel to be in constant contact, allowing the office to monitor the vessel's performance, location of equipment, and loading and discharging of cargo and to evaluate planned performance so that greater efficiencies can be achieved.

The invention of a universal barge coupling, which could be retrofitted at reasonable cost and be simple and safe to operate, would be a breakthrough in speeding fleet make-up and turnaround time.

Opportunities for increasing lock capacity exist. Lock controls could be centralized and automated. Closed circuit television cameras could expedite lockages because a person would not have to walk from one end of the lock to the other to make sure everything was in order. Separate facilities could be constructed to take care of recreational boat traffic. Impact barriers could be installed to protect gates. Double gate systems could be installed as an alternative to having two chambers. If one gate is damaged, the other would be operable without having to shut the chamber down. Replaceable fenders, energy absorbers, or rolling fenders could be installed on lock walls to prevent damage. Waiting areas could be provided near lock gates. More responsive and flexible scheduling procedures could be established and priority given to faster locking tows.

The cost of locks and dams may be reduced as new construction techniques are developed such as precasting various elements of a lock structure and/or precasting entire segments of locks and assembling them by using post tensioning and prestressing methods. Technological advances in the design of locks and dams over the past several decades have improved safety, service time, and maintenance requirements. Additional savings in this area as a result of research and development should result in improvements which will offset any increase in construction costs.

Physical modeling for waterway systems is an expensive undertaking. More effort needs to be directed at developing mathematical models for portions of the system.

Finally, ongoing research needs to be continued to extend the navigation season in the colder areas. New technologies include lock-wall heating elements, especially for locks being rehabilitated, air curtains at lock entrances, ice control by booms and other structures, coating for lock walls and gates, and protection for floating mooring bitts.

The inland waterways industry lacks organized information on which to base management decisions. During the last 10 years MarAd, through its Cooperative Industry Research Program, has funded most of the research studies conducted in the industry. Since the projects usually have the participation of industry, MarAd's programs have been guided toward commercially viable goals.

Major areas of research include maintenance and repair, advanced ship systems, market analysis, ship board automation, navigation and communications, cargo handling, energy conservation, and fleet management.

Maintenance and repair projects evaluated underwater cleaning and inspection techniques as a method of extending the period between dry dockings. Research on marine coatings and preventive maintenance has produced better rust inhibitors and anti-fouling bottom paints.

Example projects included the Vessel Vital Signs Monitoring System study which evaluated the need to obtain, transmit, and analyze vessel equipment performance data to produce decision-oriented management information to aid the maintenance department.

Another project is for better communications for the western rivers and the Gulf Intercoastal Waterway. A prototype system tested in 1985 resulted in a successful vessel to shore communication. The entire system will be capable of handling voice and data communications.

The foregoing areas of technology development and application represent a high risk if a single company attempted the work alone. However, with initial funding by MarAd and cost sharing by the private companies involved, this research was possible.

In summary, technology developments in the inland waterways sector of the maritime industry have resulted in dramatic increases in transportation productivity through vessel and barge design and operating systems. However, the current depression and overcapacity in the industry have dried up incentives and investment for further improvements. Consequently, research and development is now limited to MarAd-funded study projects and Corps of Engineers and Coast Guard projects aimed at improving the physical infrastructure. The development needs of the industry include improved management, information, and communications systems. Also, the industry needs a technical capacity for participating in developing intermodal systems.

5

CONCLUDING OBSERVATIONS ON INDUSTRY AND GOVERNMENT MARITIME R&D

This concluding section provides observations on the roles of public and private organizations in accomplishing improvements in technology development and application in the maritime industry. The most significant technology developments and applications in industry have occurred under conditions of a strong market outlook and favorable financial rewards from investment in research and development or capital equipment. Those conditions occurred in the segments of liner ship operating and marine terminals. More recently, shipbuilders have been able to achieve major productivity and management system improvements as the result of the Navy's fleet buildup, which is still underway. Finally, the inland waterways sector achieved dramatic increases in productivity through an investment in towboats, barges, and fleeting methods between the 1940s and 1960s. This investment was supported by an infrastructure provided through the Corps of Engineers, an expanding demand for movement of bulk cargos, until recently, and by heavy regulation of railroads which hampered competition, also until recently.

All of these developments were accomplished by the operating corporations in the industry, but the government played important supporting roles in each case--providing the physical infrastructure (Corps of Engineers built and maintained waterways and harbor channels) and the market demand (Navy shipbuilding and Jones Act), and facilitating technology transfer and innovation (Maritime Administration).

Incentives for industries to invest in the R&D process are strongest when they give the user a proprietary, competitive edge--e.g., cost reduction on U.S. Navy shipbuilding contracts or service advantages in international container traffic. This is because, for industry, the R&D process involves financial risk, a willingness to make substantial capital investments, or a willingness to change established management and operating structures and practices. A depressed industry is less likely to take such risks on its own.

Investors will support and make use of the R&D process when they believe it is in their business interest to do so. With sustained depressed conditions, the time may soon come when maritime managers are no longer able to justify any investment in the R&D process

because of the low level of expected return on investment. Under
these circumstances, collaborative, government-assisted R&D may become
an increasingly instrumental element to improving or at least
maintaining national productivity and competitiveness in the maritime
industries.

Much of MarAd's R&D effort in recent years has been directed at
such collaborative projects with industry. Through the SNAME it has
worked with industry to improve U.S. shipbuilding technology. With a
coalition of liner ship operators, it is supporting advances in cargo
handling technology. MarAd is also working with liner operators as
well as U.S. labor unions to facilitate the application of more
effective manning practices in U.S. vessels. These efforts have
achieved broad national benefits to the industry and the country by
facilitating technology transfer and the introduction and application
of available technology. As a consequence of these efforts, MarAd is
well positioned to continue to promote collaborative R&D within the
maritime industries.

Additionally, the MarAd should conduct substantially more R&D in
support of its own capabilities to promote the U.S. maritime
industries. It could focus on operational analysis, for example, to
better understand the effects of safety and economic regulation on
productivity and competitiveness. Similarly, impacts of structural
changes in the maritime industries should be investigated. A
particularly promising R&D area would be to provide the technical
basis for eliminating or improving regulations that adversely affect
the cost-effectiveness of the maritime industries; an example would be
analysis of the long-standing international requirement for a
dedicated radio operator on board ship and demonstration that the
requirement has been made redundant by advances in telecommunications
technology.

Finally, work performed at the MarAd-owned, contractor-operated
CAORF directly supports national requirements in harbor and waterway
development. Work performed at CAORF has facilitated the application
of simulators to, and improved the cost effectiveness of, waterway and
harbor design in the U.S. In this and other ways, the MarAd has
sought to strengthen the national capability to maintain and improve
the nation's maritime transportation infrastructure and maritime
technical capability.

Other federal agencies concerned with the maritime industries
(e.g., Coast Guard, Corps of Engineers, and Navy) have, in general,
directed resources to R&D to meet their own mission requirements.

The committee has carefully reviewed technology development and
application in the maritime industries and has shown that there are
serious concerns for the future. While the U.S. led the world for
many years in development and application of maritime technology, it
no longer does so. The modest sums available to the MarAd for
investment in R&D are insufficient for the creation of new knowledge;
they may be sufficient, however, to promote technology transfer. The
conclusions of this report, contained in Chapter 1, delineate the
roles and activities that industry and government should pursue if

technology development and application in the maritime industries are to be improved in the support of domestic productivity and international competitiveness.

APPENDIX A:
BIOGRAPHIES OF COMMITTEE MEMBERS

George F. Mechlin, Jr. has spent most of his business career working in advanced technology areas. He has been with Westinghouse Electric Corporation since 1949 and is currently vice-president of research and development and general manager of research laboratories. Dr. Mechlin is a member of the National Academy of Engineering, a member of the Commission on Engineering and Technical Systems, past member and chairman of the Marine Board, and past member and chairman of several Marine Board committees concerned with engineering safety in the marine environment. He holds masters and doctors degrees in physics from the University of Pittsburgh. Dr. Mechlin is a member of a number of professional societies and is the recipient of the U.S. Navy Meritorious Public Service Award, the Westinghouse Order of Merit, and the John J. Montgomery Award.

Daniel Brand is an expert in transportation engineering and research. He has been vice-president of Charles River Associates, Inc., since 1977. Mr. Brand has been chairman of several committees of the Transportation Research Board. He also was vice chairman of the American Public Transit Association's (APTA) Policy and Planning Committee. Author, editor, and co-author of numerous publications, he has been active in other professional activities in the transportation field. He was undersecretary, Executive Office of Transportation and Construction, Commonwealth of Massachusetts from 1975-1977. He was associate professor at Harvard University, 1970-1975, and lecturer at the Massachusetts Institute of Technology, 1969-1970. Mr. Brand has a masters degree in civil engineering from the Massachusetts Institute of Technology; he also attended the University of Vienna and the Swiss Federal Institute of Technology.

Jose Femenia is a maritime engineering educator and an expert on marine fuels and operations. Since 1974, he has been chairman of the Engineering Department at the State University of New York (SUNY) Maritime College, Fort Schuyler, New York. He is also a visiting professor at the World Maritime University in Malmo, Sweden. His research interests include marine power plant evaluation, ship vibration, pollution control, and marine fuels. From 1979 to 1980, he served on the National Research Council Committee on Alternate Fuels for Maritime Use. He is a life member and past member of the executive council of the Society of Naval Architects and Marine Engineers. Mr. Femenia holds an M.S. degree in mechanical engineering from the City University of New York (1967), and a B.E. in marine engineering from the SUNY Maritime College (1964).

Ernst G. Frankel is professor of ocean systems at the Massachusetts Institute of Technology and also ports, shipping and aviation adviser to the World Bank. Author of over 100 papers on shipbuilding, ship operations, port development, and other aspects of ocean systems, Dr. Frankel has worked and consulted for numerous shipbuilders, ship operators, government agencies, port administrations, and manufacturing companies. He has authored texts on both shipbuilding and shipping. His research and consulting interests include ship production and fabrication, naval ship design and operation, system reliability and maintainability, transport system analysis, port planning and design, transportation economics, port and coastal engineering, international shipping and shipbuilding, shipyard management, and naval ship procurement. At MIT, he teaches graduate courses in these areas as well as special courses to industry and government executives. Dr. Frankel received a B.S. degree from London University, a mechanical engineering certificate from MIT, an M.B.A. degree from Boston University, and a Ph.D. from London University. Dr. Frankel is a member of numerous professional societies including the Society of Naval Architects and Marine Engineers and the Royal Institute of Naval Architects.

Andrew E. Gibson is a shipping company executive, with policy-level government experience. Since 1983, he has been chairman of American Automar, Inc., an American ship owning and chartering company. From 1979-1982, he was President of Delta Steamship Lines, Inc., a leading American shipping company operating 24 vessels in trade from the United States to Latin America. He has also been president of Maher Terminals, Inc. (1975-1977), and Interstate Oil Transport Co. (1973-1974). From 1969-1972, Mr. Gibson served in the Nixon administration as assistant secretary of commerce for maritime affairs and then as assistant secretary of commerce for domestic and international business. He has also served as an ambassador-level international trade negotiator. Mr. Gibson is a member of the board of directors of the Panama Canal Commission and the Industrial Policy Advisory Committee of the Department of Commerce. He is also a director of the American Bureau of Shipping. Mr. Gibson holds a B.A. degree in economics from Brown University (1951), and an M.B.A. degree from New York University (1959).

William J. Harris has been involved in materials science and industrial R&D for many years. He founded the Research and Test Department of the Association of American Railroads and built this department into a focal point of planning and coordination of technical development for the railroad industry. Earlier in his career, Dr. Harris worked on materials science problems and issues while on the staff of Battelle Memorial Institute and also during his service with the Materials Advisory Board of the National Research Council. His professional activities have included membership and service with the Engineers Joint Council, the American Institute of

Mining, Metallurgical and Petroleum Engineers, the Metallurgical Society, and other organizations. He is a member of the National Academy of Engineering, and has served on many National Research Council study groups. Dr. Harris received a B.S. degree in chemical engineering and an M.S. degree in engineering from Purdue University in 1940, and an Sc.D. in Metallurgy from the Massachusetts Institute of Technology in 1948. Dr. Harris retired from the Association of American Railroads in 1985 and is currently distinguished professor of transportation engineering at Texas A&M University.

John H. Leeper is concerned with technology development and economic feasibility of maritime projects. He is president of the engineering consulting firm of Phillips, Cartner & Co., which he joined in 1985. Before that he was with Simat International, Ltd., where he directed projects on port and carrier marketing, intermodal transportation, foreign-trade zones, and port and carrier financing. He regularly validates economic and market analyses on new transportation and maritime ventures. Prior to joining Simat International, Mr. Leeper was for several years a senior project manager with the Maritime Transportation Research Board of the National Research Council. Mr. Leeper is past chairman of the Panel on Economic Analysis of Marine Transportation Systems of the Society of Naval Architects and Marine Engineers, and is a member of a number of other professional societies. He holds a B.S. degree in transportation economics from the University of Colorado (1960) and an M.B.A. degree from the American University (1967).

Frank W. Nolan, Jr. is an expert in marine terminal design and operation. He spent 38 years with International Terminal Operating Company, retiring in 1984 as vice-president of engineering and purchasing. He is currently an associate of Container Transport Technology Co., which provides engineering services and technical management support in the areas of terminal development, container handling and logistics, terminal management, and container and related transport equipment design. Mr. Nolan is past chairman of the Cargo Handling Panel of the Society of Naval Architects and Marine Engineers. He is currently vice-chairman of the International Cargo Handling Coordination Association. Past service with the National Research Council includes membership on the Committee on Ship Operation R&D and the Committee on Intermodal Terminal Design. Mr. Nolan has a B.S. degree in marine transportation from the Massachusetts Institute of Technology.

Edwin J. Petersen has 23 years' experience in ship construction, repair, design, and R&D management, and 14 years' active service with the U.S. Navy. Currently vice-president and general manager, Naval Technology Division, Todd Pacific Shipyards Corporation, he established and manages this new organizational element which was

founded to develop and promote conceptually advanced naval ship designs with emphasis on highly efficient design and construction methods. He also develops and manages the corporation's R&D program. His previous experience at Todd includes service as vice-president of programs and resources, assistant general manager, and program manager for frigate construction. Earlier in his career, Mr. Petersen was associated with Designers and Planners, Inc., and Defoe Shipbuilding Co. In the Navy, Mr. Petersen held a number of engineering duty assignments, including project management and waterfront supervision of construction and repair at naval and private shipyards.
Mr. Petersen is a member of the American Society of Naval Engineers as well as the Society of Naval Architects and Marine Engineers. He recently stepped down from the chairmanship of the Ship Production Committee of that society. Mr. Petersen holds a B.S. degree in engineering from the U.S. Naval Academy and an M.S. degree in naval architecture and marine engineering from MIT.

Milton Pikarsky is an engineer and manager with broad experience in transportation system research and operations. Currently a distinguished professor at City College of New York, other academic appointments he has held include director of transportation research and research professor, Illinois Institute of Technology Research Institute, and adjunct professor at the University of Illinois at Chicago. Professor Pikarsky has worked as a public works civil engineer, and has been commissioner of public works for the City of Chicago. He has also been chairman of the Chicago Transit Authority. Professor Pikarsky served on the Transportation Advisory Committee of the Federal Energy Administration. He was elected a member of the National Academy of Engineering in 1973, has served on the NAE Committee on Public Engineering Policy, and currently serves on the Governing Board of the National Research Council. He has also been chairman of the Transportation Research Board and chairman of the National Academy of Engineering Bay Area Rapid Transit Committee. Professor Pikarsky was elected Chicago's Engineer of the Year (1968) and Civil Engineer of 1970, Illinois Section of American Society of Civil Engineers. He has authored two books and a number of technical papers on the subjects of public works and urban transportation policy and management.

Robert N. Steiner is an expert in marine terminals and ports. He has served with the Port Authority of New York since 1967. He is currently deputy director of the port department, where he directs the planning, maintenance, operation, promotion, and development of marine terminal facilities. Early in his career, he sailed as a deck officer in the U.S. merchant marine and was employed by Sea-Land Service in the marine operations and marine terminals departments. Mr. Steiner is a member of a number of professional and trade organizations. He graduated in 1962 from the U.S. Merchant Marine Academy at Kings Point with a B.S. degree in marine transportation.

Robert J. Taylor is an expert in technology development for the merchant marine. He served in the tanker department of Exxon International Company for 20 years. He joined Exxon as a project engineer for R&D, and held a series of increasingly responsible positions including manager of R&D, design manager, manager of construction and design, and technical manager. He retired in 1985 from the position of vice-president responsible for all Exxon marine technical activities, including design and construction programs, R&D, and technical services for the operating fleet. Before he joined Exxon, Mr. Taylor was a design and research engineer with the Maritime Administration and served with the Army and the merchant marine. He is a member of the Technical Committee of the American Bureau of Shipping and is a member and past chairman of the Shipbuilding Standards Committee of the American Society for Testing and Materials. He served previously on the National Research Council's Committee on Ship Structures. Mr. Taylor received a B.S. degree in naval architecture and marine engineering from the University of Michigan (1956) and an M.S. degree in ocean engineering from Stevens Institute of Technology (1959).

John F. Wing has extensive experience in transportation systems and operations. He is senior vice-president, Booz, Allen & Hamilton, and is manager of the firm's Transportation Consulting Division. His personal consulting practice is in the maritime field, where he directs studies of economic analysis and new technology evaluation for liner and bulk fleets, market research for marine equipment, manning, development and feasibility for seaports, evaluation of barge versus rail movement, marine safety and risk analysis, and other marine-related policy, technical, and economic evaluations. Mr. Wing's early professional experience included engineering assignments with Alcoa Steamship Company and ship design with Bethlehem Steel's Shipbuilding Division. Mr. Wing has lectured on transportation economics at the University of Michigan and at Clemson University, and has presented papers for the Society of Naval Architects and Marine Engineers and the Society of Automotive Engineers. He is a past chairman of the Marine Board of the National Research Council. Mr. Wing received his B.S. degree in naval architecture and marine engineering from the Massachusetts Institute of Technology and his M.B.A. degree from Harvard University.

H. Peter Young is vice-president of marine operations for American President Lines, Ltd. He is an expert on ship operation and fleet management. Mr. Young is currently responsible for all fleet operations, maintenance and repair, fuel purchasing, vessel design, acquisition, and construction. Since joining APL in 1979, he has served as director of vessel maintenance and repair, managing director of breakbulk services, and managing director of the Taiwan region. Prior to 1979, Mr. Young spent 3 years with Seaworthy Systems as manager of marine systems. He additionally held technical positions for five years in the marine application of gas turbines and related fuel R&D with United Technologies Corporation after a 2-year stint as a licensed seagoing marine engineer. He is an engineering graduate of the U.S. Merchant Marine Academy, class of 1969. In 1972, he obtained an M.S. degree in management from Rensselaer Polytechnic Institute.

APPENDIX B:
WORK GROUPS OF THE COMMITTEE

SHIPBUILDING

Edwin J. Petersen, Leader
Todd Pacific Shipyards Corp.
San Pedro, California

John Boylston
Seaworthy Systems, Inc.
Solomons, Maryland

Jess W. Brasher
Robert Slaughter
Ingalls Shipbuilding Co.
Pascagoula, Mississippi

Ernst Frankel
Massachusetts Institute of
  Technology
Cambridge, Massachusetts

C. L. French
National Steel & Shipbuilding Co.
San Diego, California

James Lisanby
Naval Services International, Inc.
Washington, D.C.

James F. Wilkins
Kenner, Louisiana

SHIP OPERATIONS

Ernst Frankel, Leader
Massachusetts Institute of Technology
Cambridge, Massachusetts

Daniel Brand
Charles River Associates, Inc.
Boston, Massachusetts

Charles R. Cushing
C. R. Cushing & Company
New York, New York

Jose Femenia
SUNY Maritime College
Bronx, New York

Andrew E. Gibson
American Automar, Inc.
Washington, D.C.

John H. Leeper
Phillips Cartner & Co.
Alexandria, Virginia

Eugene R. Miller, Jr.
Hydronautics
Laurel, Maryland

Milton Pikarsky
City College of New York
New York, New York

John F. Wing
Booz, Allen & Hamilton, Inc.
Bethesda, Maryland

H. Peter Young
American President Lines, Ltd.
Oakland, California

MARINE TERMINALS

Frank W. Nolan, Jr., Leader
ITO Inc., Retired
New York, New York

Leo Donovan
Booz, Allen & Hamilton, Inc.
Bethesda, Maryland

Lee Lane
Bradley Gewehr
Association of American
  Railroads
Washington, D.C.

Eugene K. Pentimonti
American President Lines, Ltd.
Oakland, California

Milton H. Pikarsky
City College of New York
New York, New York

Christopher Redlich, Jr.
Marine Terminals, Inc.
Long Beach, California

Albert Rosselli
Harry Ekizian
T.A.M.S.
New York, New York

Robert N. Steiner
Michael Morrow
William Cronin
Port Authority of New York/
  New Jersey
New York, New York

David Tolan
Sea-Land Services, Inc.
Iselin, New Jersey

A. Yobey Yu
ORBA Corporation
Mt. Lakes, New Jersey

INLAND WATERWAYS*

William A. Creelman
Marine Consultant
St. Louis, Missouri

Robert Meyer
National Marine Service
Houston, Texas

*Reviewed working paper.

APPENDIX C: LEXICON

<u>Technology</u> is in its broadest sense the organization of both empirical and theoretical knowledge into a consistent and systematic entity. The entity may take the specific form of equipment or devices, but also encompasses "how-to-do," including the organization of work and also computer programs.

<u>Research and development</u> (R&D) is the effort that creates the organization of knowledge into devices or systems previously defined as technology.

The <u>research and development process</u> means the creation and beneficial application of technology.

<u>Innovation</u> is a very broad term that generally means the introduction of something new with a particular connotation of the commercial application of an idea. There is a natural association of the term innovation with the R&D process because the availability of and uses for technology are so pervasive in our society. The terms "innovation" and "research and development process" are often used interchangeably.

<u>Technology transfer</u> means the adaptation of technology into practical use independently of the source. In this sense, technology transfer is an element of the research and development process.